To Babs

My Schizo-Affective
Garden Of Eden

from Anne-Louise x

christmas 2013

Anne-Louise Lowrey

chipmunkapublishing
the mental health publisher

Published by
Chipmunkapublishing

http://www.chipmunkapublishing.com

Copyright © Anne-Louise Lowrey 2013

Edited by Laura Riley

ISBN 978-1-84991-951-7

Chipmunkapublishing gratefully acknowledge the support of Arts Council England.

My Schizo – affective Garden of Eden

In the news:

One huge difficulty I've generally had, has been keeping in touch with news and current affairs. This is largely because of the very obvious reason that it's depressing; it's all bad news and it can worry and upset me. It's also because my concentration is poor and when I'm feeling low, I tend to assume responsibility for everything that has gone wrong in the world. At the moment, with the financial crisis becoming ever more severe, I'm aware that my own survival has depended mostly on the National Health Service and the Welfare State.

I have often found it hard to form opinions about politics, society and economics, for some reason feeling that I wasn't really a fully fledged citizen because I wasn't contributing directly to the economy. However, I feel it's important to have contact with the outside world and the general mood and attitude of the present time. I still tend to do this sporadically, using internet and radio mainly, as well as watching some television when I'm visiting friends as I don't have one of my own.

I still have to be feeling quite strong to really engage with this, and while I may have expressed some sort of political affiliation, I don't really feel that I have a great understanding of politics. I usually feel quite upset by the way that politicians speak to each other, as well as the way that the press sometimes reports things. I am usually quite confused by parliamentary debates, and find that even discussions among friends can be really quite aggressive, which usually puts me off. This is when being exposed to nature on a regular basis can help to calm me down and put things into perspective. However, what I will say is, that writing has helped me to express ideas far more easily than the spoken word or any other art form, and this has been my main motivation for writing these poems.

The meaning of life

Humble bumble bee
Are you a person,
Just like me?
Earwig, woodlouse, snail
And wriggling
Arachne-that-I'm-phobic-about
How much I wonder about you
Basic instincts are your only perceptions
Yet vine-weevil
Are you aware,
Just how annoying you can be?

Butterfly, I'm content
Not to have your beauty
But just to feel
Its ecstatic effect
And ladybird
I just want you to be my pet
Wasp, are you a Communist,
Or a Royalist?
What's your view mother earth worm
On the conflict in the Middle East,
The financial crisis, the hacking scandal
And the meaning of life?

The mighty that have fallen

We can reveal
All the swingers, the spankers,
The paedos and the sado-masochists
All the scroungers and the undesirables
Living in your area

You see that lonely looking man
He's probably just out of prison
Or a psychiatric hospital
No woman, few friends
There's definitely something suspicious about that

But we knew nothing about this scandal
We were all so shocked
That we're doing the decent thing
Closing down, but still there in spirit,
Upholding the values that we all hold so dear in
society

But don't you fret, we're not deserting you
We'll find a way to keep you in touch with the real
zeitgeist
The gossip, the outrage and the tittle tattle
And of course, for extra special entertainment:
The mighty that have fallen

And don't worry lads
There'll still be plenty of tits
Not those tree hugging hippy types though,
Who breastfeed on the bus
That's disgusting; it shouldn't be allowed

But nice, naughty, nubile thirty six double F
Twenty four waist and thirty two hips
Smooth, toned, hairless and always smiling
That's the way your woman should be lads
So just give her a slap if she's not.

New Rose

The bride was really, really pretty
And the Prince was very, very handsome
And a new rose was born
I don't really mind if you're a wild rose
A climber or a thornless rose
An old garden rose
Or a modern hybrid

As long as you're not really really hung up
About how very, very beautiful you are
And you're not just another image
That's going to look down on me from afar
And be so concerned with the clothes you are
wearing
And the photographs that are taken
That all your good intentions are swallowed

In a world of really, really important appearances
With very, very significant people
And all the crowds who come to cheer you
Are just faces, uglier than yours
And less meaningful than those that
You mingle and mellow with
On these magnificent occasions

What the earth could be

Ok Fred, you were the demon knight
Ok Fred, bully for you
Ok Fred, now you're in the limelight
And you're not alright

On top of the world the air is thinner
You need to come down gradually
Or spend time in a decompression chamber

Even a private jet
Is just a temporary tin can
That's grounded sometimes
And it will wear out eventually
And be melted down
And could be made into trident missiles
Or ambulances, or washing machines
Or earrings for New Look and Primark

I've got a different story
Kicking and screaming
I was dragged into an asylum
Against all my protestations
That they had made a terrible mistake
I wasn't mad; I was actually the whore of Babylon
The beast with seven heads and ten horns
I didn't need medication
I just needed petrol and a box of matches
To burn the heavy lumps out of my soul
The hunch off my back

And all the warts and boils
That were invisible to the unenlightened

And I'd have to spend a million years in purgatory
To make up for the damage I'd caused
But somehow they didn't believe me
And they drugged me anyway

I hadn't eaten or drunk for over a week
And my body went into spasm
They held me down to stop the shaking
And gave me a glass of lemonade

They managed to crush the delusions and
fantasies and terror
But they crushed everything else as well
And the whore still re-emerges from time to time

I was told that my weight could easily spiral out of
control
That I might develop Parkinson's
And that I had a chance of tardive diskinesea
(Involuntary movements of the head and tongue,
Caused by irreversible nerve damage)
I would find it hard to concentrate on anything
That I would probably never be able
To make meaningful, lasting relationships with
people
Or have children
That I was unsuitable, incapable of employment
And could really only do occupational therapy
If I ever went to college
I would probably be bullied

And passes would be a bonus
I was ridiculed by people
And sometimes regarded with fear
A possible danger to others
Jealous weak and inadequate
Over sensitive and paranoid
I just imagined that people were being unkind
I should lower my own standards and expectations

I was twenty two

But now I'm a liar and a cheat
I've pretended to be ill all these years
Using up resources
Recklessly causing a credit crunch
And creating a world recession
So I'm just as responsible for the demise of the
global economy
As you are Fred

Of course we bad apples flourished
Under the previous Government
They gave you a knighthood
And me my first job
And a few more rights
Than free range chickens
And a chance to meet people
Outside the asylum
And somewhere to go
When the whore rears her ugly head
That isn't little more than a punishment

I took on too much Fred

And bit off more than I could chew
So I've got something in common with you

I think you're a tosspot Fred
But there's nothing folk like more
Than a worthy scapegoat
And there's nothing more attractive to power
Than manipulating the masses

So maybe we'll both go to purgatory for a million
years – or longer
But I reckon it'll be pretty crowded
With members of the previous Government, the
present Government
Jews, Muslims, Christians, Hindus, Buddhists,
Scientologists
Lap dancers, vicars, professors, homemakers,
and royal families
The list is endless
But there'll be no euro or dollar or pound there
No credit cards or benefit claims
No rising interest rates, no job losses
No recession, no credit crunch
So there'll really be nothing for us to talk about
And maybe we'll learn to stop arguing
And make it into a pleasant place
A little bit like heaven
Or what the earth could be

Mental Health:

I suppose I have quite a lot to say about this, but not necessarily always in an angry or desolate way. The main symptoms I have day to day are feelings of anxiety, depression and paranoia. This whole collection pertains to mental health, mental illness and stress but hopefully it is not too bleak. I often feel low and negative and find that writing my thoughts and feelings down help to alleviate this. I have a keen interest in holistic health of the body and mind and environment, which is why I am so happy at Redhall, but often become frustrated with my own addictions mainly to caffeine and nicotine. I've an extreme tendency to become lethargic and untidy at home and often find it hard to settle into a Tai Chi or meditation session, which I know would be much better for me than a cigarette.

Writing is a good therapy for this, as it's not a particularly messy hobby and although it keeps me up late sometimes, it's good for the concentration and can be energising. It is difficult for me to become engrossed in anything as even sitting still for any length of time can be a trial when you are taking anti psychotic drugs. It's a relief to sometimes forget myself, even if it's only for 10 minutes or half an hour at a time.

I've tried to address and hopefully understand emotions like anger, hopelessness, fear and blame, trying to find some positivity through the experience of these generally quite stressful moods, but at the same time acknowledging that they are there. Gone unchecked, I found that I was experiencing psychosis and needing more medication during periods when I was angry or afraid. I am now finding ways to release tension more healthily by writing things down, as well as by taking part in the gardening work at Redhall.

The Pavement
When I was young
I thought that superstars
Would drink and drug all night
They'd sleep all day
With nothing to pay
That would make the slightest dent
On their bottomless bank accounts
At every opportunity
Their opinions they would vent

And nowadays I look around
And see the wasted genius
Young lads and girls
In doorways, begging
For people to be lenient

And as I sit at home, relaxed
I know I've paid my rent
With legal drugs, I know it's true
I'm just as much an addict too
And one step off the pavement

Someone to blame

The pain in my head is not your fault
Mother, father, spouse, brother sister
Doctor, teacher, manager, nurse
Prime Minister, Friend

But you can help it to be less daunting
Less debilitating, less frightening
Less hurtful, less unhealthy
You can help

By not thinking of me as a poor soul
That you need to be stronger than
By not thinking of me as being lazy
And a drain on resources

By not being jealous of what is right with me
Of the things I achieve
By not favouritising me
But being uncaring about others

By being truthful
And encouraging me to do the same
But it will never happen
There will always be someone who finds someone
to blame.

New Leaf

Once I've turned over a new leaf, I'll be up to scratch
There'll be no weeds in my garden
And my lawn will be perfect – all the time

All the corners in my house will be dust free
All the glasses will be sparkling
And all the clothes will be hung up or folded away
– ironed

I won't smoke and I'll just have a moderate drink at Christmas
I'll cook every evening and exercise every day
Every morning I'll eat breakfast after my Pilates –
fruit

I'll never be out of work and I'll have scintillating hobbies
I'll learn languages and start to travel
I'll have no cellulite and start to run marathons –
for charity

I won't gossip or worry over trifles
I won't compare myself to other people
And think that they've had it easier than me –
even if they have

On the other hand, I could go and buy some Chardonnay
Some crisps, chocolate and tobacco
Invite Jenny and Nancy over – and just have a
right good chinwag

Imagination

When I'm in depression
I can't really cry
There's something in my chemistry
That makes me want to die

My forehead's thick and furrowed
My shoulders ache like hell
I cannot find its reason
It's like a witches spell

But sometimes when I fantasise
About a healthy me
I find a ghost of happiness
And imagine being free

And then I start to look around
And notice little things
Like raindrops on the windowpanes
And my auntie's wedding ring

And beneath the dust of my neglect
Throughout these tortured years
I feel the love that's filtered through
And somehow find my tears

And when I feel that weight relieved
I venture from my bed
And find a way to tell myself
That this is in my head

There's no one I will talk to
As often as I should
To help me out and find a way
To understand these moods

I've tried a lifetime to do what's right
For society and me
But more frequently than I can count
I've failed quite miserably

So the only thing that I can do
Is to find this little light
Called my imagination
And believe that I'm alright

Then perhaps I'll eat some bread and cheese
And make a cup of tea
I'll wash the mouldy coffee cups
And brush my yellow teeth

And then I'll toddle back to bed
To nurture energy
And find the strength to face the cloud
That's reigned so long in me

No man's land

Thank God for anti psychotics
And therapeutic art
And nature, music, literature
Philosophy and family spats

The Tory Party conference
Gets off to a gleeful start
There will always be those
Who don't like me
So I shouldn't take it to heart

Sometimes I feel it was wrong
To ever be young and idealistic
Caring only about love and peace and fulfilment
Aspiring to be an artist or a mystic

Not particularly worried
About lung cancer, breast cancer
Or cholesterol
Was I an Anarchist, Socialist, Pacifist?
Would I be different,
If things had been different for me?

Would I still be worried about the young,
The old, the vulnerable?
Are the politicians as concerned about them
As they say?
Am I as worried about them as I feel?
Or simply vulnerable myself?

As fond as I am of Vincent Van Gogh

His sunflowers
And crows over a cornfield
His potato eaters
The romantic tragedy of his life

I don't really aspire
To be a romantic tragedy too
Thank God for anti-psychotics
And some sort of selfish way through

Far from being a perfect solution
And not a miracle wonder drug
They've simply saved me so far
From the clutches of the institution
And no man's land

Enigma

Something's pushed my panic button
The alarm's been howling for days
I cannot tell you what it was
It's one of those enigmas
I'd like to just erase

Perhaps there's not enough of me
For all I'd like to do
I'll make a cup of herbal tea
Analyse the situation
And think and think it through

A tear jerking tune
Repeats and repeats in my mind
Please don't take my man Jolene
I'll never love again
Please don't leave me behind

But apart from all this pleading
With beauty and love and providence
Why me? What for?
Will I lose everything?
Or will I gain some recompense?

The end is the beginning
Or so the Bible says
But who can understand it all?
From burning bush to Pontius Pilot
We're really all just strays

So one enigma leads to another
As the mysteries of life unfold
And who knows what tomorrow brings
Should we just fall fast asleep
And say that it's been foretold?

Huff

I'm as angry as a prostrate toddler
Lashing out with their arms and legs
Red and ugly with rage
Thrashing around in contortions of temper
Feeling cornered and afraid
A tantrum about not getting their own way

Yet you know nothing about this
As I sip my coffee
No food in my belly
And I'm simply not hungry
For the casserole you've made me

I'm frozen and polite about it
Coldly making myself a sandwich
And eating it disinterestedly

Just now, I don't really care
Whether you still think I'm beautiful
Despite my denture, my menopause
And my descending bust

It's my denture, my menopause
And my bust

When you come near me
I know I'll be ticklish to your touch
Maybe giggling a little
Maybe frowning
Maybe squirming and screaming
Lashing out with my arms and legs
Irritated by your good humour
Annoyed that things haven't gone to plan
A tantrum about not having got my own way

I sometimes think

I sometimes think
That the world
Would be better off
Without a shirker like me

Working with the soil
And living free
And the beasts I encounter
Mice, spiders, wasps, and an array
Of flora and fauna
Kindling love of life
And creating a peaceful aura

If it wasn't for me
And my singing in the woods
Dancing round the campfire
And wearing walking boots

Shopping at Shelter
Oxfam and Age Concern
Outdoor and camping shops
And visiting farms

Looking out for otters in the dell
And setting off on wild treks
In the hope of seeing badgers
Before the cull

And learning Latin names
For all the birds and trees
Planting herbs and flowers
To encourage bumble bees

At least without this, people would be able
To watch television in their homes
Without the constant pounding
Of environmental drums

Surely it's better, if you're going to volunteer
To do it at Poundland, Primark, Asda
That will further your career

And at least there'll be somewhere
For folks to spend their hard earned money
And a lot of people don't really like
Mice and spiders and wasps
They're happy to sit on the patio
And complain that it's not sunny

Anne-Louise Lowrey

Happy to be Happy

What's going to happen,
To my limbs as I get older?
Will they twist and swell?
Will I be hunched at the shoulders?

Will my mind become brittle?
My extremities sag?
Will I look frail and little
Clutching my handbag?

And what of my brain
Which I rarely use?
Will I still be insane?
And will I be excused?

And what will become of our galaxy?
The moon, the stars and sun
Will they still be here
When I'm old and done?

A mayfly lives
Just one human day
And doesn't seem to mind this
It's just happy to be happy
And simply float away

Inspiration

From inspiration comes creativity, and there are lots of people and situations which can inspire us. I find nature inspirational and certain moments in life but I've also tried to pay homage to some of the people who have really lightened my load and assuaged the hopelessness that I often feel. The depressive side of my illness can be really overwhelming, causing sleeplessness, suicidal thoughts and difficulty interacting with others. I don't always find it easy to express optimism or have a spring in my step every day, but some people really make me want to improve things, and just appreciate life more.

I used to find it disconcerting when I heard about those who had accomplished great things in the face of adversity. I suppose I felt inadequate, because I couldn't even seem to stay on top of the housework, or catch the early bus to work, or deal with any kind of awkwardness in my life very easily. But now I'm beginning to realise that I have achieved some things, and even managing to stay out of hospital for a number of years is something I can be proud of.

Working in the garden has been a turning point and as well as giving me occupation and friendship and support, it has also provided a kind of spiritual sustenance and increased my determination. I can honestly say that there is not a single person I have met at Redhall who has failed to inspire me.

Peaks and Troughs

The traveller comes breezing
In from the east
15000 kilometres
From Chiang Mai to the Athens of the north
Forms a bridge across a void
No less than an odyssey on two wheels
Where countless peaks and troughs
Have been conquered
And not with nothing to lose

Do you know about suicide?
About the peculiarities of the body and mind?
About agony and inspiration?
About ecstasy and nature?
About love of life
And having fun?
Missing your mum and dad
And seeing them again?
Making new friends
And cherishing old ones?
About drinking a cold glass
Of Irn Bru?

My deep blue mood is lightened
By the excitement
And a discombobulation
Of home made banners and pink balloons
Well dressed kids
And scruffy grown ups
Some yummy sandwiches

And rather an oversized cake
I don't really like parties
But this one has a life and soul
The star attraction as self-effacing
As we are proud of her

When the main thing I'm really certain of
Is that, with invariable regularity
I'll wake up bristling all over with fear and dread
and gloom
The familiar abyss that never ceases to shackle
me
Then there's little left but the unknown

Which is beginning to look more interesting
Even slightly attractive.

There are sometimes, those who pave the way,
Build roads for others to travel on
Abi you've done just that for me
I'll probably never cycle across continents
But I might just be able to get up in the morning
A little brighter and a little earlier
Listen peacefully to my own will's desire
And embrace the life of day

Valentine

I'm not a star
No moon-travelling, astronaut,
Rocket scientist, supermodel,
X-Factor finalist, best-selling,
Internet sensation, celebrity,
Royal.

No double first student
Athlete, yummy mummy
Domestic goddess, entrepreneur,
Yogindra, philanthropist
Survivor.

But I do twinkle
When I see you
Standing clumsily
In my doorway
Your soft-eyed,
Mischievous smile

My sweet as a packet of raisins
Cute as a Schnauzer puppy,
Loveable as Looby Loo

And I hope that we can brave
The weather together
Find some space
Among the clutter
Be at home and abroad
With each other
And maybe sparkle sometimes

The first frost

I'm glad to hear the music
Of the river through the trees
The dogs barking
And children running free
I can see frost on yellow fungi
Forget-me-nots
Teasel, bulrushes, and frozen rosehips

Hibernation is underway
And I've the whole winter to enjoy
I'll come back here every day
And feel the same, timeless happiness
As my senses I employ

Birds still serenading
Through the leanest times
Cyclists whizzing past
Through avenues of limes
Great hawks and buzzards patrol the skies
It's the perennial joy of change
As the old season dies

Anne-Louise Lowrey
Putting the world to rights

Is there something out there?
Or something deep within?
Two for one lasagne
And a bottle or three of wine

A night out with the girls
One of my favourite things
Long lingering conversations
Fake fur, perfume and bling

False tan, religion
Cellulite and the economy
Politics, weightwatchers
World Peace and ballet
Celebrities, terrorism
Medical ethics and shoes

Wimbledon and worldwide want

There's more to girly chats
Than reputation would have us believe

But do sociology and bargain hunting
Really complement each other?

Clothes and glamorous trinkets
Are all made in sweat shops
By ragged children
So we can look our best
Great ugly factories
Where workers rarely eat or rest

My Schizo-Affective Garden of Eden

Cotton growers starve
While we worry ceaselessly about fat
And the size of our jeans
Trying to defy age and gravity
With push up bras
And body firming creams

You only live once
And we're not too vain to care
But how do you put the world to rights
And somehow make it fair?

I'll take a taxi home
To avoid the stag parties
And rowdy late night clubbers
Throw my clothes on the floor
And my shoes in the cupboard

Then I'll get my Avon brochure
And choose myself a treat
I'll telephone it to my friend
And arrange a time to meet

I'll mark it in my diary
As a very special night
When all us girls will congregate
And put the world to rights

Home and Dry

The hot blisters pulse painfully on your stump
It feels raw, just like your memories
You find it hard to remember what happened half
and hour ago
Yet, the past ten years are another story
Your story

A youthful prank has left an indelible mark
You didn't intend it to be like this
What could you have done?
Where would you be now if she hadn't told you to
jump?
You jumped

Electrician, teacher, bus driver, father, doctor
The list is endless, just like your medical
appointments
You've had to spend your time simply coping
As for the girl of your dreams, she's somewhere
else now
You're dumped

Some of your companions are twice or thrice your
age
The women you seek are experienced, not
frivolous
Yet you always manage to smile sweetly
Living each day without resentment
Are you home and dry?

Where animals live

Everyone's in
With a shout I'd say
Don't wait indoors
For a warmer day
There's more to be gained
From work and play
Than not enough money
To keep bills at bay

I look to myself
For space in my head
And friends for agreement
And sharing the dread
That makes us worry
For our wine and bread

There are still some places
Where animals live
And people can go
To restore and forgive
The forces that we
Ourselves must survive
And the people that
We sometimes despise

So don't laugh at me
When I say
I'm off to the woods
To forage and stray
Because everyone's in
With a shout I'd say
We've created our own society

Sonja's Brunch
Croissants and bacon
Contentedly taken
The morning after they came to stay
There's orange juice too
And a continental brew
With pickles, tomatoes, cheese, fish and ham

Oatcakes and butter
To do us till supper
With death by shopping in-between
I miss her smile,
Her straightforward style
I even miss her temper, her energy, her accent

It's always a bummer
When marriages flounder
And you end up losing a friend
She's gone her own way
And doesn't come to stay
And breakfast just isn't quite the same.

But what if?
In the dimness of the small hours
I meditate upon my woes
And muster up excitement
As my faulty strength grows

The spring is coming closer
And afternoons will stretch
And pregnant queens will forage
Starting to build their nests

But what if

We have a later snow,
Or a heavy frost?
Then daffodils will perish
And lambs will be lost

So let's think of what will flourish
In the coming weeks
Will humankind ever have
The certainty it seeks?

And who decides what wisdom is
As we activate our plans
On farms, in cities, villages
And all our different clans?

Should we succumb to nature,
Though wild and untame?
Or should we just remember
That it's from whence we came?

Let's relax

Even I relax sometimes, usually because I've become so intensely anxious, that it has to dissolve sometime. Dilemmas about life, worries, regrets, faith or lack of it can all provoke disquiet and even a feeling of powerlessness. Here are just a few poems I wrote, mostly when I was sitting up late at night, knowing I wouldn't be able to sleep and just beginning to feel my mind starting to work overtime.

Lullaby

Tonight, don't think of things you haven't done
Or things you feel you'll never do
Or crave for love that never was
Or blame another for the things you rue

Don't even pressurise the Gods
To save your gentle, mortal soul
Or bring you fortune, faith and hope
Or give you strength, or make you whole

Don't tire yourself by praying
For peace and harmony on earth
Just sleep, and be these things yourself
As naturally you were at birth

And when you learn just how to be
Without the pain of what is past
Or wanton fear of what's to come
Then you are with yourself, at last

And remember that your industry
Is worth as much as any other's
And remember that you live on earth
An equal to your sisters and brothers

Jesus' Heart

Jesus, I've got such a soft spot for you
I hear you've conquered death
But can't you help me to conquer life?

You claim that there will always be life
That there's a time for war and a time for peace
But can't we just have peace?

All powerful and ever living God
Who sacrificed your son
How many sons have been sacrificed in holy
wars?

You say that the poor will always be with us
Should we constantly toil and spin
Or should we consider the lilies of the field?

Your evangelists have spread the word
Since ancient times, from distant climes
But what now, all these martyrs later?

You'll always have a place in my heart, Jesus
I hope I have a place in yours
But would you mind very much if I moved on?

Peace on Earth

I've been searching for loving kindness
And I've found it in the pound shop
Christmas tree decorations
The supermarket oranges
And the shortbread I bought
From Harvey Nic's as a present
But decided to eat myself

On council estates and country estates
In the compost heap
And out by the wheelie bins
In the deep fat fryer
And on the allotment
In public houses
And in places of worship

But mostly I've found it
In my own weakness
My own shortcomings
Mistakes, feuds, personal demons
Regrets and anger
In my enemies and friends

When the wild stallion stops to rest
And the foals are at play
The mares watching over them
Then regrets are a lesson, demons ideas
Anger is energy and feuds, just rivalry
Weakness is honesty, mistakes, quite ordinary
And shortcomings melt into virtues

Anne-Louise Lowrey

Enemies and friends become people
All living in the same world
Perhaps striving to be significant
I'm looking forward to a peaceful Christmas

January

The winter sunset is early
It eases my fears away
The stark trees turn to silhouettes
And evening swallows the day

It's not a time for worry
Though what time really is?
My life is not going well just now
I'm lacking vigour and zest

But January skies, though gloriously grey
Like our complexions and emotions
They give us time to rest and pray
And nurture new devotions

So don't tire so soon of winter
As the new year scuttles in
March will be wild with wind and hail
Resolutions will be in the bin

So let's enjoy our wine and cheese
And walking in the icy breeze
And lighting scented tealights after dark
Warm and cosy, sitting by the hearth

The human condition

This is something we can all enjoy and suffer from at the same time. I suppose I still have some way to go in really understanding and accepting human nature and all its apparent cruelties and frailties. Ironically, as someone who is frequently incapacitated with depression or worry – or even joy at times – where I neglect my other duties, I have spent my life, trying to be happy and stable. Often looking with envy and awe at people who appear to have achieved this balance, or trying to help those who appear to be suffering or at odds with the world. Reading through the poems, I realise that I have expressed opinions that I didn't know I had, but most of them are just an attempt to make sense of the confusion that I feel. I believe this is possibly a safer way for me to express myself that sitting with people in a crowded pub, where I might encounter aggression, or disagree with someone and be too afraid to say so.

There are a variety of different viewpoints, all of which have a root and a degree of validity, so it's not as if I expect everyone on earth to agree with me. Most people work very hard and can become impatient with someone who is 'mentally ill' or a 'volunteer,' especially if it is a side of life that they are not familiar with or fear, or view as simply weakness. I suppose I would like to educate people as to what mental illness is, and find new and innovative ways to be healthy in a modern society, where things move at faster pace than ever before, and perhaps community isn't as strong as it was say, fifty years ago. Nowadays the statistics are one in four, so mental illness touches most people's lives in some way at some time, whether it's themselves or someone they know. It is important for people to find some common ground with each other, and this is what I have tried to achieve through writing this section.

I have learned a lot through working at Redhall, and how life can be made better through work and rest and creativity, and to some extent feel that I am on my way to achieving more of my long sought after balance than ever before. At the same time, I also realise that sometimes, by just allowing myself to be myself, the level of effort required, simply to live in a calmer way, is not as superhuman or impossible as I had previously thought.

My Limbo Garden of Eden

I'm in my limbo garden of Eden
Desperately trying
To resist temptation
To sleep among the buttercups
And be drenched in morning dew

I want to cover my nakedness
With animal skins
For my clothes and shoes

And take the honey from the bees
And till the soil and fell some trees
And train the wolves
To do my dirty work
And milk the cows
And feast on pork

So perhaps I'll take this golden fruit
From this forbidden tree
And see what God's reaction is
I'm dying to be free

And I know I'll hanker back a lot
To when I was this child
Living in God's cradle
Where everything was mild

But the spirit of adventure
Will always win me through
The path of learning for myself
Is the only thing that's true

But there's something in God's garden
That makes me want to try
To re-create his Eden
On earth where I will die

And then I'll feel my father's wrath
For every law I flout
I'll have to say, "I'm sorry God,
I just had to find it out."

Not completely hopeless

When I grow up,
I'm going to be overweight.
A chocoholic
And a yo-yo dieter
An obesity statistic

When I grow up,
I'm going to be an alcoholic.
A Pino Grigio-phile
And a chain smoking
Drug user

When I grow up,
I'm going to be an adulterer.
A sexaholic
And a lying, cheating
Fraudster

When I grow up,
I'm going to be a workaholic.
A negligent spouse
And parent
A lonely divorcee

When I grow up,
I'm going to get into debt.
A shopaholic
And a Jimmy Choo collector
Then become bankrupt

But whatever I become
When I grow up,
I'll still be the same child
That I am now,
Running round the garden,

Looking for my pet hamster
That I've lost.
And I'm not
Completely hopeless
That I'll be re-united with it

Anne-Louise Lowrey
The Female Fashion Factory

When I was a child
Twiggy was still on the scene
Strutting around on spaghetti legs
And youth reigned free for a while
Hotpants, mini skirts and pre marital sex

Soon came liberation for women
Wide flares, no make up, hairy legs
Birth control, college, men with pony tails
Goat's milk, muesli and free range eggs

Then it was time
To take the kid gloves off
Shoulder pads, killer heels
The make up was back
Along with promotion, home ownership
HRT and business deals

You can never be too rich or too thin
The industry becomes full to the brim
Credit cards mean luxury for plebs
People without are pushed to the edge

Now the polar ice caps are melting
Capitalism is in crisis
And our cities' hearts beat with social unrest
 A magazine asks us:
"Should politician's wives champion British fashion
designers,
In tough economic times?"

Perhaps they should remember
That clothes were invented
To keep us warm in December
And cool in July
And cover our modesty
And keep us dry

And women fought hard to have a voice
Equal pay, education and some sort of choice
And surely after all we've been through
From suffragette to boardroom etiquette
We can say that fashion is fun
It's a wonderful form of art
But there's much more to a woman
Than paying through the nose
And silently looking the part

Anne-Louise Lowrey

Ugliness is in the eye of the beholder

Look at her! What a dog
She thinks she's twenty and she's forty
Hey! Lardass, can I shag you?
Mind you, you'll have to pay me

Look at him. What a dog
I honestly think there should be a law against
Overweight, middle aged men
Wearing shell suits and football strips

If I looked like that
I'd invest in a home gym
And never leave the house for six months
Until I was fit to be seen again

You can't play with us, you're a dog
You've got buck teeth, cock eyes
A spotty face
And you're mum buys your trainers from Asda

Yet, take a walk down the park
And the brutal looking Bull Terrier
Cavorts freely with the
Baby faced Labrador

The Poodle isn't worried about his hairstyle
Or his Pekinese girlfriends cheek bones
Or the price of her collar and lead
He's just happy to see her

The Chihuahua isn't afraid
Of the Rotweiler's bulk
And the massive Bull Mastif doesn't feel too
clumsy
To stand next to the sleek Doberman, or the
graceful Setter

So the next time you're having a bad hair day
Or you're feeling old or fat or stupid or just crap
Or someone calls you 'Hey, Rover'
You're a cow, horse face; in fact you're an ugly
dog

Just think that it's not such a bad thing
To be like a dog
Because a grey haired, thick waisted, middle aged
Heinz fifty seven
Is just as happy as a pampered, champion,
Afghan hound

Free to be free

Familiar sight, familiar noise
The geese are migrating
Strange people, strange customs

All this human order
And disagreement
Some wear veils, some mantillas
Some turbans, some bowler hats
Some skull caps, some bikinis
Some study rocket science
Or devote their lives
To fathoming out
The natural order of things

Some spend lifetimes,
Nurturing personal grudges
Some hate themselves

Some eat animals, drink wine
Some live on fruit and nuts
Some natural omnivores
Some eat each other

Sometimes shooting each other
Torturing, and burning each other alive
Sometimes singing and dancing
And procreating together

Sometimes hurting or humbling themselves
For penance or pleasure

Yet we say that nature, and Arctic weather
Are often harsh and unpredictable
We feel we must protect ourselves from them
Thinking that animals,
And the extreme conditions they inhabit
Don't have souls or know God
The way that humans do
They don't have self control

An ever reforming arrow
Slices across the sky
In perfect co-operation

Some geese will be lost on the way
Like stonemasons falling to their deaths
From a great monument or cathedral
Their purpose and creativity
Dying with them
Their imaginations gone

But the wild flock escapes
The farmer, the butcher
The gourmet chef
The roast potatoes
And the Christmas dinner plate

It escapes the human order
And lives in a dwindling pocket
Of harmony and freedom
Amid the chaos
Of the monuments and cathedrals

Anne-Louise Lowrey

Not suffering until,
The Arctic is a sea of mud
The Rainforest an arid desert
And the English country garden
An ice-packed tundra

Because of human order
And its great feats
Of industry and engineering
Its monuments and cathedrals
Its everlasting wars and disagreements

This is our family
Free to be free

Age and Beauty

Smoking kills
It also makes your teeth fall out
When you're in your forties
Your face looks crushed
Your fingers brown
And you generally look dirty

And as I shop around
For my Tena Lady
Thermal underwear
And denture fixative

I marvel at my fellow women, and men
Who've managed to avoid these afflictions

And I carry on regardless
Of pain, fatigue and ugliness
I hope that I can still reach them
And not become repugnant

But the world is as
It's always been
And age is rarely equal to beauty
Especially when it's premature
And because you've been quite naughty

Human Rights

Virginia tobacco
Cannabis
Opium poppy
Cocaine

The prehistoric animal
Stands erect
And poisons itself
For the sake of its enormous brain
And immortality
And resistance to pain

Chilli peppers
Marinated olives
Espresso coffee
Darjeeling tea

All things
Of relatively little interest
To the wild stag
Or the fishes of the sea
They don't prize these things especially
Or need them to quell their boredom

Like Homo sapiens
Caged in by comfort
And progress of a sort
Looking to escape the cold
The midday sun and the rain
With tasty things to excite their brain

Vines from Bordeaux
Cocoa from Ghana
Barley
And hops

All cultivated for human entertainment
Yet we're still no tamer than the raging bull
That charges the fence
To get to the cows
Because that's his nature
But what's human nature?

Irritability with creativity
Anger and sadness with love
Both hunger and gluttony bring equal pain
Some tortuous journeys seem completely in vain
The luxury of thinking
Of experimenting

With plants, and tools
Medicines and weapons
Will the cannabis and cocaine
Pacify a charging rhinoceros, or a raging bull?
Make them smile and dance to the dawn chorus?
Do these animals somehow think that whisky and
beer

Will make them more attractive
To the opposite sex?
Do they need chilli peppers
To make their food more interesting?
Coffee to wake them up in the morning?

Tea to calm them down?

Do they need tobacco to help them concentrate?
Wine and olives to occupy themselves
Or break the ice in company?
Opium, because life is just too difficult
And the pain of mere existence
Is simply too great to bear?

I'm not sure that they believe
In fairies, or witches
Ghosts or leprechauns
Angels or mermaids
Deities or devils
Nor are they blinded by science

Yet they seem to understand
The world they live in
And get along just fine
They don't seem to want immortality
Wealth or fame
Cattle, cockroaches, pine martens

Penguins, stingrays and skylarks
They don't need us
To provide them with food
Or water or shelter or love
They don't need books or temples
Or prisons, or paintings or pasteurised milk

Or fashion, or fuel
Or perfume, or email or TV
It's great to be a homo sapien

But it's also great to know
That we're almost surplus to requirements
And without us
There would be no damage,
To plants that make oxygen
To the ocean's living wealth
To the insect population that pollinates the flowers
That produce the fruit
That feed the animals

The human animals

And now we need our wilderness
More than ever
To teach us that we've no more right
To be here than a dandelion
Or a dung beetle

Our souls are no greater
Or more entitled to eternity
Than a sewer rat
Or a sunflower
Or that unemployed layabout who lives round the
corner

Being Alive

A baby kitten
A dormouse
A darting swallow
A ladybird
A dragonfly
A newt

All small or furry
Beautiful or cute

But what about an angry wasp
An adder in the grass
A German Shepherd running loose
A spider in the bath?

A hungry rat
A scratching cat
A vicious stoat
A butting billy goat?
Are they all reminders
Of our ancient urges?

Somewhere far away inside
At the back of our heads somewhere
Surely a purpose resides?

The goal of happiness
Is possibly higher
Than fame or monetary gain
Or simply burning in life's fire

So when we're faced with a growling dog
Or a giant cockroach under the sink
Is it time for fight or flight?
Or is it time to stop and think?

Are we tolerant of other forms
Of life apart from ours?
Or are we losing everything
In pursuit of other powers?

And should we halt our progress
In this ever faster race?
Are we heading for Utopia
But can't keep up the pace?

And what about a flatter tum
And more expensive shoes?
A holiday three times a year
One-upmanship with friends and foes

The worry over children's schools
Our mortgages
And staying within society's rules

And will we let our family down?
Will they embarrass us?
Sometimes we want to run away
And indulge our wanderlust

And when we view our world at war
Starvation, pain and fear all over

We sometimes find it hard
To pull ourselves from bed
And all our good intentions
Are frustrated in our heads

So if I can't find a dormouse in the woods
Or a swallow free and graceful in the sky
Then I'll make do with slugs and snails
Tarantulas and slithering eels
Rotweilers, centipedes and scavenging gulls
Because they still remind me I'm alive

Just for fun

There is room for fun, even in my life and it's something I believe to be as important as a work or study or debate or philosophy or money. It makes a huge contribution to health, and while there are a lot of serious and important issues to be contended with, it is also important to relax sometimes and find things to enjoy just for the sake of it. I am learning that I can face some of the more difficult things in life, if I just stop worrying about them and have some carefree time, where I am not so conscious of myself, or any kind of viewpoint or mental illness, or low self esteem or unachieved ambition. I am simply who I am, where I am right now.

Food is of great enjoyment to me, and even though I can be too disorganised to cook, I manage to sometimes and also take pleasure in a microwave meal or a takeaway which more often than not ends up being a curry because of its comforting and antidepressant qualities. Another thing I like is being out of doors, and I am becoming used to all kinds of weather, including the much berated British summer. Since I've been working as a gardener I've enjoyed all the seasons, but especially the summer, which I used to moan about, along with everybody else when I worked in an office. I always seemed to get caught in the rain when I was walking to the bus stop, or popping out for a sandwich. Now I tend to think of it as being quite warm and sunny, as it doesn't actually rain all day long. When you're in a garden, you always catch the sunny spells as well as the downpours. I find myself chuckling a little when I hear people's complaints, as I can remember doing the same thing myself. My own garden can be a bit neglected sometimes, but I have fun with my brother and my dad in their allotment and garden, often misplacing gloves or the odd hand fork. However, when my dad's boots went missing, it gave us all something to laugh about.

Hot Date
It's November and I'm alone tonight
Bob Marley playing on my laptop
I'm about to indulge
In a very tasty love affair

A bit of alright

My husband knows about this
The third person in the marriage
A unisex pleasure
That we both agree on

A hot date when we're together
Company when we're lonely
For each other

Rummaging around the desk
Looking for a menu
Sometimes the freezer
For a supermarket special offer

Sometimes the cookbook comes out
And the spices are ground,
The herbs home-grown
Sometimes a jar of paste is utilised

Whether it's chicken, meat, prawns
Broccoli, lentils or chickpeas
Dopiaza, jalfrezi, pathia
Rogan Josh, Bhuna, or Tikka Masala

Anne-Louise Lowrey

There's an aphrodisiac in every bite
Joy by mouth

If you've ever tasted
Neck of mutton stew,
Ox liver casserole, or tripe
You'll know what I'm talking about

British summertime

I wouldn't call you lazy
But you just don't seem to try
Your long blonde hair and big blue eyes
Strawberry lips and rosy cheeks
An abundance of inherited wealth

Yet often you are sulky
We can always depend on you to cry
At weddings, picnics, festivals
For whole weekends and camping holidays
During lunch breaks, barbeques and tennis
tournaments

You're a disappointment golden girl
A temperamental brat
After all the hope we've invested in you
Why can't you just smile when you're supposed
to?
We've had so many complaints about your attitude
and behaviour
Of course, things were different when I was young

The Riveting Riddle of Charlie's Boots

Charlie's boots have gone astray
To be found in odd places
With the laces all mangled and frayed
Underneath the whirligig
Behind the cabbage patch
What would be thief
Has done this deed
And never tried the latch?

Is there another
With such muckle feet as these,
That a pair of fine quality,
Vintage tackity boots would please?

So Charlie is bemused and confused
On closer inspection
He thinks these laces have been chewed
What cunning carnivore
Has created this incredible hoax?
The conclusion seems to be
It was a hungry little fox